Animals at Night

by Althea
pictures by Gary Rees

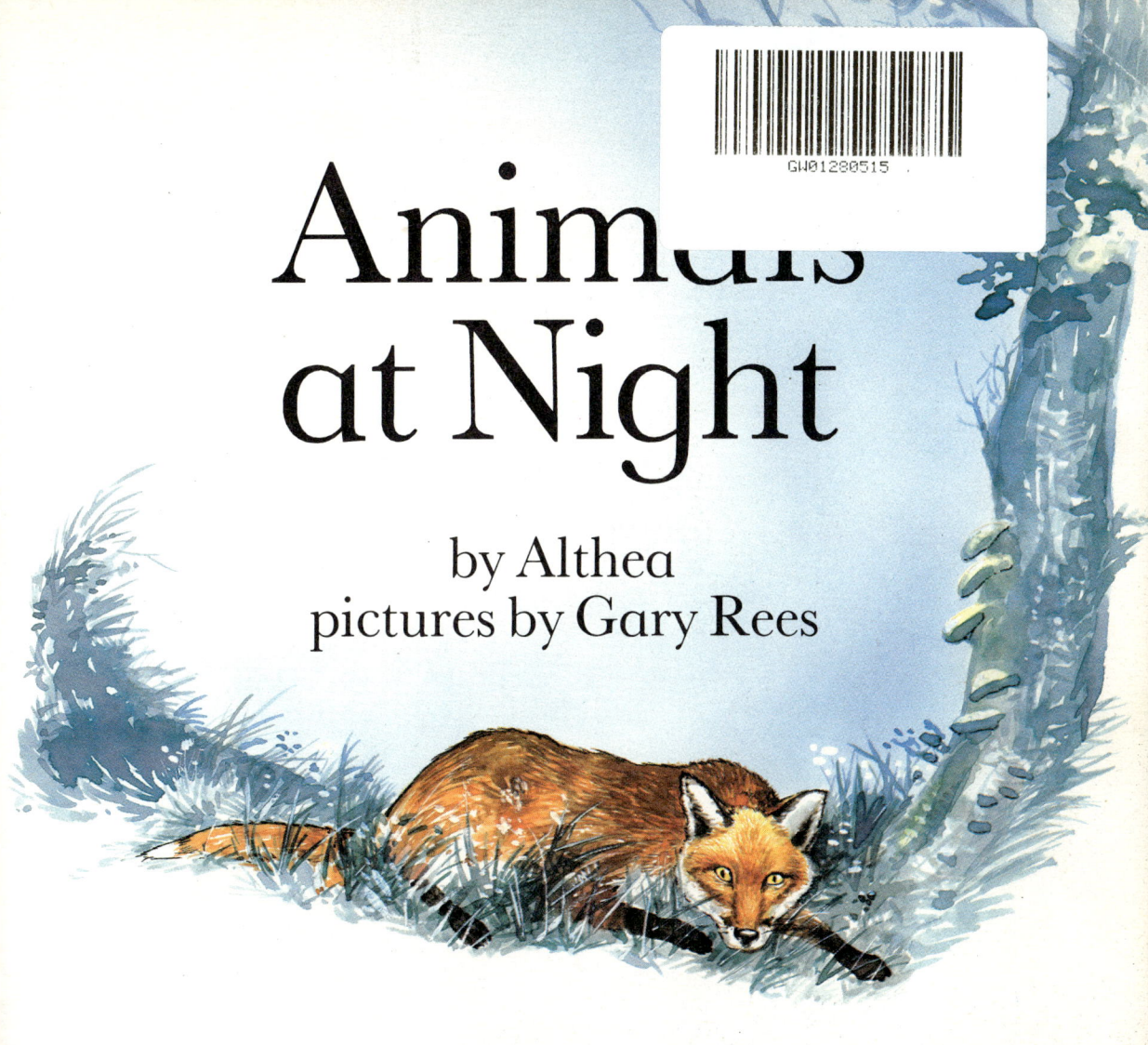

Published by Dinosaur Publications

As it starts to get dark
at the end of the day,
many animals come out
of their hiding places.

Rabbits come up from their
underground home, called a warren,
to feed on farm crops and
grass in the meadow.

Hares rest by themselves during the
day, hiding in the long grass, and
come out to feed at dusk.

Bats circle in the sky,
swooping to catch flying insects.
Bats can fly at great speed
without bumping into one another
or anything else.

As they fly, they make high pitched
squeaks that echo back and
give them a 'sound picture'
of where they are.

Lacewings and some moths hear
the bats and fall to the ground
to avoid being caught.

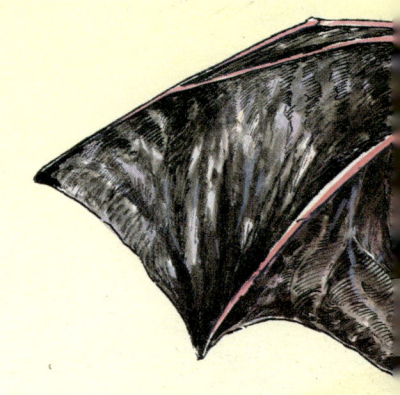

Flowers like the honeysuckle give out their scent in the evening to attract moths to them.

The Hawk moth unrolls its feeding tube to suck the sweet nectar from the depth of the honeysuckle flower.

In the cool damp of evening,
frogs and toads come out from under stones
in search of a tasty meal.

Frogs have a long tongue, which they
flick out to catch flying insects.
They also eat snails, slugs and worms.

Slugs and snails search for food at night.
Their tongues are covered with thousands
of tiny teeth to chew leaves and plants.
They return to their home in the daytime
to keep damp and avoid being eaten
by thrushes and other birds.

Worms slide out of their burrows to
collect dead leaves for food.
They keep their tails in their tunnels
so they can shoot back in at great speed
if they hear danger approaching.

Badgers love a meal of worms and may catch several hundred in a night. They also eat young rabbits, slugs, grass, fruit and nuts.

They can't see well but they have a very good sense of smell.

They dig large underground homes, with lots of passages and rooms where several families may live together.

Early in the year, male and female foxes call to one another at night as they look for a mate.
They prowl around in search of food and will catch and eat young rabbits or chickens as well as mice, beetles and worms. Foxes living near towns scavenge in dustbins.

Wood mice scurry about leaping up
into bushes to look for fruit and nuts
to eat. Some of the food
will be stored for later in their
underground homes
or in an empty bird's nest.
Their huge eyes help them
to see in the dim light.

A Barn owl flies silently through the night ready to glide down and pounce when it hears a wood mouse rustling through the leaves. It eats birds, beetles and even frogs.

The Barn owl's shrill scream warns other owls to keep off its territory.

Some animals need the cool damp of night to move around in. Others feel safer in the dark, and many find it a good time to hunt for food.

As day breaks, they will all return to their homes to rest.

Text copyright © Althea Braithwaite 1987
Illustrations copyright © Gary Rees 1987

Published by Dinosaur Publications
8 Grafton Street, London W1X 3LA

Dinosaur Publications is an imprint of
Fontana Paperbacks, part of
the Collins Publishing Group
Printed by Warners of Bourne and London